Winning at the Capital Game

Using Other People's Money (OPM) to Build Wealth

Capital Raising – Your New Superpower

www.bradblazar.com

Copyright © 2021 Blazar Group, LLC

Acknowledgements

This book has had so many hands involved in the process that there is no possible way to thank everyone who has contributed. First, I'd like to thank my wife Shelli and daughter Brooke who have been an inspiration. They have seen my coaching and consulting business grow from scratch to a point today where we serve people around the world. For both me and them, that's exciting. Their belief in me doing something BIG and finishing this project helped me keep on track – despite the long hours and late nights. To Marko Markovic, who designed the cover of my first book *On the Wings of Eagles – Learn to Soar in Life* which became a #1 top rated read for young entrepreneurs on a major literary blog and who contributed to this books design as well.

To my personal coach and mentor, Micheal Burt who a few years ago activated something in me he refers to as "prey drive" and allowed me to step into my bigger potential.

Thanks to the great leaders in business, politics, and sports whom I have either met, or had the pleasure of working with – perhaps sharing a stage, hosting them on my podcast or collaborating on a special project. You've inspired me and have helped me grow.

And lastly, thanks to my family from my mother and siblings who have been in my corner each step of the way.

Other books by Brad Blazar

On the Wings of Eagles – Learning to Soar in Life

Put Some Thrive in Your Hive
Unlocking Potential in Any Organization

Both Available on Amazon

Note to Reader

The information shared in this book comes from the experience I've gained over 30 years raising capital and money from investors. It started in my 20's as the former CEO and founder of a small oil company I started that grew over 10 years with drilling projects in multiple states.

Fast forward, I've now raised more than $2 Billion dollars through my efforts and the efforts of teams I've led for multiple top real estate and financial services companies in addition to setting the records for largest transactions in many cases - $11M for USAllianz, $9M, $7.5M, $5M and more for SmartStop Self Storage and more. Serving private equity firms, Wall Street financial services firms and more has given me an excellent framework from which to write this book.

Additionally, I've funded real estate deals and transactions as General Partner or co-GP over the years which largely contributed to the knowledge in writing this book for you.

I hope you enjoy reading and more importantly get a better understanding on how to successfully raise investor capital.

A portion of the author's profits from this book are being donated to charity and cancer research

Table of Contents

Introduction — 6

Chapter I – Starting advice from others — 9

Chapter II – Why investors don't sign NDAs — 14

Chapter III – What investors are looking for — 19

Chapter IV – How to prepare before you pitch — 26

Chapter V – Types of funding available — 33

Chapter VI – Different types of investors — 44

Chapter VII – When do investors invest with you — 48

Chapter VIII – How to pitch to investors properly — 58

Chapter IX – Closing the deal – getting a check — 79

Chapter X – Advice from professional investors — 84

Chapter XI – Industry Terminology – things to know — 90

Introduction

Having raised $2 Billion dollars in investment capital in addition to closing the largest mega-million dollar transactions for real estate sponsors and financial services companies like SmartStop Self Storage ($9M, $7.5M, $5M and more) as well as USAllianz ($11M) I can tell you I know a thing or two about raising capital and using OPM (other people's money) to build, buy, or scale a business – or fund a special project like real estate. Learning how to raise money in my 20's allowed me to build a small oil company and today run a global business teaching others how to do the same.

This book is largely designed to share with you MANY of the things I have come to know about raising money from investors, family offices, RIA firms, broker/dealers and more. Raising capital isn't easy, BUT it can be done and more importantly it is a skill that can be learned.

Investors that fund startups or invest in things like real estate syndications range broadly – from high net worth (HNW), family offices, VCs as well the function they provide (start-up versus coming in at later funding stages). They include high net worth individuals looking to diversify their investment portfolio beyond the traditional securities markets and banking products, and fellow entrepreneurs or early employees of a startup who've done well on an exit and want to dive back in. They are former entrepreneurs and business owners, they are product engineers from tech companies, they are retired hedge fund managers living on boats in the Virgin Islands, affluent doctors and more. They provide access to much needed capital necessary to bring ideas from the lab bench to traditional brick and mortar retail, and from the whiteboard to the mainstream - when no other source of funds is viable.

Seen at times as a necessary evil, and others as brothers-in-arms in the fight to survive, grow, and thrive, they are quite certainly a critical component of "start-up-dom." Typical perception among the early-stage entrepreneurial community is one of an adversarial chess match played between hard working entrepreneurs, bathed in blood sweat and tears, defending their equity from robber baron investors who want to take a majority equity position and run the company. It's not the case that this is never accurate, but it's certainly not the norm.
Investors are instrumental to startups. I created this guide because navigating the various, nebulous sources of information on the different types of investors, where to find them, how to approach them, what they are looking for, and what turns them off, can be a frustrating and challenging process.

Who Should Read This?

I wrote this investor guide for startup teams and entrepreneurs who want to engage in raising funds from investors to launch and scale businesses. My hope is that it will serve as a trusted advisor and North Star as you embark on your search for capital.

What You'll Learn in the chapters ahead:
- Chapter 1 : Starting Advice from the Trenches
- Chapter 2 : Why Investors Don't Sign NDA's
- Chapter 3 : What Investors Look For
- Chapter 4 : What To Prepare Before You Pitch
- Chapter 5 : The Types of Investor Funding
- Chapter 6 : Types of Investors
  and so much more…

Chapter I
Starting advice from others

When you're a startup entrepreneur or small business owner, you're all about ideas.

You have a plan to make the world – or some small part of it – better, whether that's more efficient, more equal, more convenient, or just more fun. You've spent months, years, maybe even decades of your life with your idea: researching, refining, revamping, reimagining, and all the while dreaming of the day that those ideas finally materialize in the real world.

By the time you get to the point where you're ready to launch your first investor fundraise, that day is so close you can practically taste it. After all, investors have the one thing that stands between you and transforming your dreams into reality: capital. Investors provide over $100 billion to startup companies every year. And they are idea people, too: passionate about helping good ideas get off the ground – even if that passion shares the stage with a concern about bottom lines.

But despite the essential role investors play in the lives of startups, there are surprisingly few quality resources for entrepreneurs to turn to in order to get reliable, straightforward information about investors, what they look for, and what entrepreneurs need to do in order to successfully earn their support.

My goal with this guide is to change that, starting with some good news and some bad news.

Good News and Bad News

The good news is that now is an incredible time for startups to connect with investors that share their vision. The internet has created and continues to create new ways for entrepreneurs to reach out to investors, and the passing of the JOBS Act in April 2012 and the subsequent rise of crowdfunding has forged new pathways to investor wallets.

The bad news – well, not so much "bad news" as simple fact – is that investor fundraising still takes a lot of work. It's a grueling, time-consuming, at times frustrating process. If investments were made in companies based on merit alone, the world would look a whole lot different than it does today. The fact of the matter is that there are a lot of other factors that go into investors' choices of which opportunities to invest in and which to let pass.

The purpose of this investor guide is to demystify the investor search somewhat, and to help entrepreneurs put themselves and their businesses in the best possible position to get the support they need. Before we dive in, here are a few thoughts to carry with you through the chapters to come.

Know Your Business

It will become clear pretty quickly as you proceed through this guide that a lot of the investor search process—the kinds of investors you'll pitch to, how you'll structure your fundraise, what your crowdfunding profile will look like – depends on the particulars of your specific business: industry, size, stage of development. Before you get the ball rolling on reaching out to investors, be sure that you know where you stand on all of those items, and that the needs and goals of your company are clearly defined.

As an entrepreneur, you are your company's best advocate and its biggest cheerleader. Nobody knows your business better than you do, and that's a strength that you'll want to play to as you pitch to investors. Be clear with investors about who you are and what your vision is. That's the fun part of pitching to investors, after all: getting the opportunity to introduce your company and make other people as excited about it as you are.

Practice Makes Perfect

As I've touched on already and will touch on again in the course of this guide, investor fundraising is a time- and effort-intensive process. You're going to put a lot of hours into preparing your materials, refining your pitches, and researching, contacting and pitching to various investors, and you may not see the payoff for those efforts right away. It may be weeks before an investor responds to your email, or before you land your first in-person pitch opportunity. You may hear "no" from investors dozens of times before you finally hear your first "yes".

But it's vitally important that you don't become discouraged when investors aren't immediately lining up to write you a check. Keep in mind that raising funding isn't about finding just any investors: it's about finding the right investors for you and for your business. Each rejection brings with it an opportunity to strengthen your business plan and improve your pitch for the next time around. Be patient, be relentless, and be ready to learn throughout the process.

There Are No Guarantees

The goal of this guide is to give entrepreneurs the tools they need to successfully pitch their company to investors. That is not to say that entrepreneurs that follow the advice outlined in this guide are certain to get their funding. If you're looking for a foolproof checklist – "Do this, this, this and this and you're 100% guaranteed to get funded" – keep looking but be warned: you'll be looking for a very long time.

When it comes to investor-based fundraising, there is no such thing as a sure thing. Every investor – and every company – is different, and so is every fundraise. I have compiled a collection of pointers and best practices to get you as far down the road as I can, but at the end of the day you are your own best resource. The more information you seek out, the more you prepare before launching your fundraise, and the more proactive you are throughout the process, the better your chances are of seeing the results that you're looking for.

What You'll Find in This Guide

This guide is designed to help entrepreneurs navigate the tricky waters of finding, contacting and presenting to investors. We'll touch on a number of different topics related to that process in the chapters to come, from the kinds of things investors look for in a potential investment, to the materials you'll need to prepare before you talk to investors, to pointers for preparing pitches to investors across different formats. We'll also provide some resources and tools to get you started in the fundraising process and answer some frequently asked questions about investors and investor-based fundraising.

My hope is that this guide will help you to orient yourself and your company within the sometimes bewildering process of raising capital from investors, and point you in a direction – or several different directions – that will lead you toward a successful fundraising experience.

One Last Thing…

Again, the road to investor-based funding is a long one. It takes time, it takes work, and it takes determination to get an investor's attention, and then keep it through the numerous stages that lead up to the ultimate goal of securing the check. When you're right in the thick of it, it's easy to get disillusioned, and lose sight of the reason that you decided to subject yourself to the whole ordeal in the first place.

So as a final piece of advice before we plunge into the guide: keep your eye on the prize. Remember that the reward at the end of this long, arduous process is getting your company or project the money it needs to thrive, and seeing your vision come to life. And that's an idea worth holding on to.

Chapter II
Why Investors Don't Sign NDA's

There's a popular misconception amongst first-time entrepreneurs that sharing a mere idea without having a signed Non-Disclosure Agreement (NDA) in place will lead to your own version of The Social Network, wherein Mark Zuckerberg (played by Jesse Eisenberg) steals the Facebook idea and becomes a billionaire.

This mythology is horrifying and persistent, but it differs greatly from the reality. Here, we will cover why investors don't sign NDA's and how stubbornly requiring one can kill your chances of raising capital.

No One Wants (Just) Your Idea
"It's not about ideas. It's about making ideas happen." Scott Belsky, Founder / Behance

"Ideas are commodity. Execution of them is not." Michael Dell, Dell Computer

Investors want entrepreneurs, not ideas. Anyone can come up with a great idea, but very few can actually pull them off. In the global marketplace, an elegant solution to a painful problem is just an opportunity, and opportunities are a dime a dozen. It's everything that comes after the realization of opportunity that turns it into a viable business; meaningful traction, a great startup team, solid social proof, the list goes on. These are the things investors' dreams are made of.

It's not that Mark Zuckerberg just happened to steal an idea for social networking. It's that he was the most capable person to actually pull it off. He wasn't the first to market (Friendster, anyone?) or the first to achieve success.

A clever idea may pique an investor's interest, but that isn't worth getting ahead of yourself and demanding a NDA. You've got plenty of other hurdles to jump.

Don't Make Life Harder

A typical investor will review upward of 20 deals per week, or over 1,000 deals per year. Signing an NDA could potentially prevent them from having a

meaningful discussion with any potential investment after yours.

Should they choose not to invest (and most won't) they would be stuck with the liability of a legal contract with you that prevents them from finding more deals. There are literally no benefits to the investor in signing your NDA.

Now, imagine you're an investor sifting through hundreds of deals. You find one that looks interesting and you reach out. The startup responds by saying you must first sign a NDA.

Do you go through the hassle of signing a NDA or do you just move on to the many other startups who aren't asking for a document that no one ever signs?

It's hard enough to get an investor to pick you out of the crowd. Don't make your life harder by insisting that they sign a document that they don't need to, don't want to, and by all accounts, won't sign.

You Can't Enforce It

The strength of any legal instrument is directly related to your ability to enforce it. Do you plan on suing investors in the near future? Do you think the power of the document you've asked them to sign will give you adequate grounds to enforce that suit?

Probably not.

Focus on what you can control, which is what information you show them and what aspects of the business you are willing to share.

Share The Cookie, Not The Recipe

If your idea is so easily stolen that just hearing the concept is enough to allow anyone to replicate it and launch it better than you, then you've already lost.

There is little protection in just a concept, so — unless you've got a secret recipe behind it — signing an NDA doesn't do you much good anyway.

You should be able to openly share the concept idea with anyone, since once your business is up and running it'll be out there for all to see anyway. If there is a secret recipe behind the concept, then by all means don't share that until you've gotten to know the investor better.

Very few ideas have a secret recipe, however, and you're more likely to be explaining why you can defend this concept once it's launched.

What To Really Worry About

All of that said, there are some things you should consider protecting as you shop your idea around to investors.

Investors who have investments in similar companies to yours could present a challenge. You are essentially providing them with competitive information that they are free to share with their other portfolio companies. Most investors will decline meeting based on those grounds in the first place.

The other thing to worry about is the dissemination of your information. Pitch decks and business plans can get shared incredibly easily. An online data room or profile allows you to grant and revoke access online, allowing you to control who sees what. Alternatively, you could present important documents strictly in person, on your own laptop.

If you're going to worry about anything, worry about actually getting a meeting with an investor. You're going to have plenty of challenges in attracting investors — don't make forcing them down the NDA path one more reason to not get a pitch to begin with.

In summary, if you're going to worry about anything, worry about actually landing a meeting with an investor. There are plenty of inherent challenges as you work to attract investors — don't create yet another hurdle by forcing potential investors to sign a pointless document.

Chapter III
What Investors Look For

It's the question at the forefront of every entrepreneur's mind as they start seeking the capital to fuel their idea: "What are investors looking for in an investment opportunity?"

The short answer is that every investor is different, and each has their own set of criteria. Some may base their decisions purely on the facts; others might be more inclined to factor their feel for the people at the helm into the equation. Some may be in the right frame of mind for risk-taking; others might be playing it safe for a while or waiting to see how out-standing investments play out. That being said, there are certain across-the-board factors investors will take into account when evaluating opportunities, and it's in your best interest as an entrepreneur to cover these bases before approaching investors with your pitch. Here, we will take a shot at breaking down what investors look for.

The Right Fit

As an entrepreneur, you're looking for investors that are the right fit for your business, and investors are looking for essentially the same thing in reverse: businesses that are the right fit for their investment portfolio. The best way to determine whether your business is a good match for investors is to look at investments they've made in the past and see whether there's symmetry.

"Most VCs will go through a checklist, and everything's got to meet our criteria. If we're vegetarian, we don't want to see a steak."
Bob Rice
Investor

Location, Industry, and Stage of Development

Are you looking to move your baking business out of your home kitchen and into its own location in Indianapolis? That's great, but don't reach out to a Seattle-based private equity company that only invests in technology companies with over $20 million in revenue. As you do your research, look for investors that are near you geographically, have a history of investing within your industry, and typically invest at the same stage of evolution that your business is currently in.

Market Size

One of the biggest variations from investor to investor when speaking to VC's, private equity shops and "professional money" is the size of their fund, and again, it's important that you find investors with a fund size that matches the scale of your business and your goals. A million-dollar venture capital fund that needs to generate large returns can't spend time on a $50,000 investment in a restaurant, no matter how successful that restaurant may be. And if you're looking for a million dollars to take your business national, is it really worth your time to pitch to an investor who can only spare $25,000?

All else being equal, targeting a large market is the best way to inspire excitement in investors. Investors will have few qualms about passing on an investment that will struggle to grow beyond a million dollars some day; but an opportunity elegantly addressing a billion-dollar market is one that even the most cautious investor will consider carefully.

"Market size matters because most investors want to know that you've got a big business. Bigger is generally better."
Dave McClure
Founder

Do Your Homework

As your own best and biggest advocate, it's up to you to do your due diligence in research and seek out the investor-partners that make sense for your business. If you shirk your research responsibilities and start pitching to random investors in the completely wrong sphere, it will be a waste of their time, sure; but more importantly, it will be a waste of yours. The more closely your business aligns with a potential investor's investment history along the axes listed above, the more likely your pitch will be to meet with a warm—or, at the very least, constructive—reception.

More Than a Good Idea

Like a proud parent, you know that your business is one-in-a-million. But the reality is that, if you've done your homework and sought out the right investors, there's a good chance that they've seen your idea—or something like it—before. And that's okay! It's the nature of the beast: a problem presents itself, numerous people try to solve that problem, and sooner or later one or two of those solutions rise to the top—and they may not always be the first ones, either. What do the one or two solutions that survive have going for them? It's not just a good idea: it's a good idea plus a critical mass of proof that that idea is going to make it out of the idea stage and into the real world.

A Competitive Edge

If an investor is familiar with your industry, they probably know of at least a few competitors for your business, and if they don't already know, they can find out quickly. Before they invest in you, they will want evidence that you have some significant advantage that the competition cannot easily overcome.

"Another misconception is that VCs like to take risks. That really

isn't true. VCs like to not take risks and bet on sure things."
Dave McClure
Founder

Maybe you have unique relationships in your industry that enable you to cut deals with partners that no one else can match. Or maybe you have a unique patent on a new product that can secure your position as a market leader for years to come. Look for some key leverage points in your business model that will convince investors that you can build a sustainable competitive advantage, and touch on those virtues early and often.
The goal isn't to prove that no one else will ever compete with you; again, the reality is that somebody probably will. The goal is to prove that when somebody does try to compete with you, they'll lose.

Social Proof

"It's become so sexy to pitch to investors nowadays that people forget to first go talk to customers. I have people pitch me, and when I ask what customers think about this, they tell me they don't know. So why are you talking to investors right now?"
Paul Judge
Founder and CTO

It's one thing if you and your mom think your idea is a good one: it's another thing entirely if Business Insider or Yahoo News runs a piece on it, or if Bill Gates is a fan. Social proof is an idea most of us are familiar with, but it's rarely outlined in a business plan or presentation. Simply put, "social proof" is clear evidence that people who are in a position to know believe in your vision as much as you do and will testify to the merits of your business.

One way to go about building social proof is to assemble a team of advisors that are well-respected in your field and have spent time with you and your vision. Another is to generate some early activity with pilot customers who will provide testimonials, not only that your product makes sense, but that if it existed today, they would buy it.

"I always look first at the people, and that covers from the customers to the entrepreneur to the team. Second is the product, because when you start a business, it's a hunch, it's a guess, and you have to go out and find out if people really want it or are you just a solution in search of a problem."
Gary Sprirer
CEO

Investors see thousands of pitches, so they often defer quickly to social proof if it provides compelling evidence that respected people have spent the time and attention with your product and are excited about it.

Traction

There are a lot of great talkers in the world, but at the end of the day, it's all about the follow through. Investors hear hundreds of entrepreneurs talk about their ideas, but very few of those ideas yield results. So, one of the best ways you can stand out from the crowd is to provide proof that you're going to hit the ground running—or that you already have.

"When it comes to business, there is a simple scorecard. Are you making money or are you not making money? Are you succeeding or are you not? So, when you go to raise money, always, always catch yourself and eliminate the backstory."
Mark Cuban - Investor

Signing up early customers, hiring key talent, or actually building your product by bootstrapping resources are all positive signs that you're resourceful and determined enough to make things work, even without substantial capital. Every bit of traction matters in a startup pitch, so however modest it may seem compared to your overall ambition, don't be afraid to touch on it in your presentation for investors. The farther you can come on your own, the more likely investors are to think to themselves: "If they can do that much with so little, imagine how effective they could be with my money behind them!"

Credibility is All

Again, there are no hard and fast rules when it comes to investors' criteria for making an investment. But if you want a single, concrete takeaway from this, here it is - investors want incredible ideas helmed by credible entrepreneurs. They're looking for good ideas to get excited about, with a solid foundation that proves it won't all wash away and take their money with it.

A final thing to remember is that investors are also people, and you shouldn't be afraid to approach them as such. Ultimately, investors are going with their gut in investing in businesses just as much as you are in creating yours. So why not give them something to believe in?

Chapter IV
What to Prepare before the Pitch

A good fundraising effort requires great supporting documents. Once you have the basics down, it's pretty easy to prepare all of these documents as needed. Here's a comprehensive list of what you'll need to prepare when you're ready to initiate your money raising efforts

Elevator Pitch

An elevator pitch is a short, consistent synopsis of your business, usually in just a few sentences. Perhaps surprisingly, getting your pitch to be short and consistent can be pretty difficult. Although the amount of content you need to create is tiny—just a few sentences—the amount of thought that goes into it is extraordinary.

A good elevator pitch conveys a few things quickly: the problem you solve, the solution you provide, and the people you do it for. For example, "We allow anyone to easily get a ride from their cell phone" would have been a succinct and effective elevator pitch for Uber.

You will use your elevator pitch often — in introduction emails, in presentations, and yes, actually in elevators during chance meetings. Keep rehearsing it and keep it short. It will inevitably prove very useful.

"If you're constructing a way to present your story, you should be aware that most investors have small attention spans. They may be late to the meeting with you, they may be reading other stuff on their iPhone. So, you want to organize your information in a way that allows them to process it more efficiently."
Dave McClure - Pitch
Founder

Pitch Deck

Your pitch deck is your business plan translated into slides, typically in a PowerPoint document.

While a business plan tends to be a long narrative of the business intended for one person to read on their own (which rarely happens—but more on that later), the pitch deck is what you'll use to present your concept directly to a room of investors or to an individual.

The pitch deck is often requested by investors ahead of your presentation so they can get a quick synopsis of your idea, so be sure to have it prepared and ready before you start contacting investors.

Unlike an executive summary, which is also a summary of your business plan, the pitch deck tends to be more visual, highlighting a few key points very well. It's particularly useful when showing off graphs and visual assets that help communicate the value of your idea.

Executive Summary

The point of your executive summary, as the name implies, is to briefly summarize your business plan into just a few pages. Make no mistake though, it's effectively the sales pitch for your business. Not only are you communicating the mechanics of the business, but you are also selling the value of your idea.

The executive summary tends to distill each key area of your business plan down to a paragraph or two, so that investors can get the gist of your plan easily.

There are two schools of thought on the executive summary. One suggests that you should write your entire business plan and then summarize it in your executive summary. This makes obvious sense; however it overlooks the fact that many people start companies without writing an entire business plan.

The alternative, then, is to try to summarize all the key points of your business clearly in a few pages, using a standard business plan as your guide.

Whichever path you choose, the executive summary will be helpful to have on hand for those investors that want a slightly more detailed narrative behind your elevator pitch.

Business Plan

It may seem as though entrepreneurs must prepare a business plan before approaching investors, but in reality actually few do.

There are a few reasons for this. First, authoring a 50-page manifesto on how your future business will operate is typically the domain of MBAs and academics, and entrepreneurs rarely have the time, resources or desire to dive into a project of that scope when they just want to get their business launched.

The second is that it's an incredibly time-consuming process if you really want to dig into every step of a business plan from start to finish.

That said, it's also an invaluable exercise.

The real value of a business plan isn't in the actual document itself — it's unlikely anyone will ever read it. The value comes from the planning, brainstorming and research that goes into crafting the plan. The result of this effort makes your assault on your new business idea far more credible.

If you decide to build your entire business plan, you'll certainly want to have it handy, but make sure if you're introducing yourself to investors you start with more digestible documents like an executive summary or pitch deck. This is a nice teaser that will prompt a request for a business plan if you've piqued their interest.

Website

Not every business absolutely needs to have a website in order to pitch for capital, but it is highly recommended. Your pitch assets tend to be things you'll either print or attach to an email. What the website provides is a reference point that provides supporting information for people who are interested in learning more after hearing your pitch.

You don't have to put your company's financial forecasts or secret sauce on your website. You can save that information for more personal communications.

The website should serve as a virtual brochure for your company. That could include screenshots of your product, a short explanation of what you're setting out to do, a personal blog discussing your thoughts on the industry, etc.

What's important about the website is that it gives people a professional view of your company, along with a taste of who you are and what you're trying to accomplish. Your website is a convenient destination for anyone — both investors and consumers — who want to know more about your company. Plus, it's much easier to direct people to your website than to a document.

Financial Documents

If everything is going well, you're going to be asked for your financial documents. These should cover a few aspects of your business, from your revenue forecasts to your operational expenses to your cash flow.

The complexity of these documents can range from a single slide in your pitch deck showing some baseline guesses on where revenues will come from, to highly complicated Excel docs that involve macros and formulas changing outcomes based on key assumptions and scenarios.

For general purposes you'll need to cover at least a few aspects of your financial picture.

Revenue Projections: You'll need to explain where your revenue is going to come from, and within what periods. A four-year revenue projection is a good place to start. Of course, no one really knows exactly how much revenue is going to get generated in the years to come, so this is more an exercise of what's possible, not what's guaranteed.

Operational Expenses: As the company grows, it's critical to point out where your expenses will grow accordingly. This is where you will explain how staffing, product costs, marketing and overhead (rent, supplies) will scale with the growth of your business.

Cash Flow: The value of this information tends to vary with the type of business. Seasonal businesses, for example, will have particular cash flow concerns when they are heavy on cash in one period and light on cash in another. Similar to your revenue and operational expense projections, your cash flow should detail exactly when you expect cash to come in and out of the business.

You may be asked for additional information such as a balance sheet, pro-forma income statement (a fancy word to mean "projected" revenue and expenses) and others. As long as you're communicating the three main tenets of the business — revenue, expenses and cash flow — you should be in good shape here.

Summary

It is possible to start your capital raising without all of these documents in place — it's just not as advisable. The documents require you to do a lot of homework and preparation, which is exactly the kind of exercise you need to go through in order to become more fundable as a company.

Chapter V
Types of Funding

When it comes to funding a business, investor-based fundraising is just one option among many, including rewards-based fundraising, personal investments, friends and family, and good old-fashioned bootstrapping. Before you decide to seek funding from investors, it's important to be certain that investor support is the best—or only—way to move your business forward.

Once you've decided that pursuing investors is the right route for you, you have another choice in front of you: how are you going to do it?

There are three basic types of investor funding: equity, loans and convertible debt. Each method has its advantages and disadvantages, and each is a better fit for some situations than others. Like so much else about the fundraising process, the kind of investor-based fundraise that is right for you depends on a number of factors: the stage, size and industry of your business; your ideal time frame; the amount you are looking to raise and how you are planning to use it; and your goals for your company, both short-term and long.
In this chapter, we'll explore each investor-based funding option in some detail, looking at the way each option is structured, situations in which each option is the most useful, and some advantages and disadvantages that entrepreneurs should keep in mind when deciding whether to choose each option. Keep in mind, though, that this is just a quick overview: you'll need to do more digging of your own before you're ready to say for certain which method is right for you.

EQUITY

Pursuing an equity fundraise means that, in exchange for the money they invest now, investors will receive a stake in your company and its performance moving forward.

Equity is one of the most sought-after forms of capital for entrepreneurs, in part because it's an attractive option — no repayment schedule. It also provides for high-powered investor partners — and in part because it's the form of capital that requires the most seeking.

How It Works

At the outset of your fundraising process, you set a specific valuation for your company—an estimation of what your company is worth at that point. Based on that valuation and the amount of money an investor gives you, they will own a percentage of stock in your company, for which they will receive proportional compensation once your company sells or goes public.

EXAMPLE: The founders of Shelli B's Sweets have decided to turn their business into a national chain, and they're looking for $500,000 in equity investments at a company valuation of $2 million. Venture capitalist firm ABD invests $250,000, earning 12.5% equity in Shelli B's Sweets.

When to Do It

There are several situations in which an equity fundraise makes the most sense or is the only real option for a company.

When you need a LONG runway

Not every business will start generating income as soon as it launches but spending a few years in the red doesn't mean your company isn't a viable business proposition - or much more than viable. Internet companies, for example, are notorious for going years in operation without even attempting to charge their customers. If you're going to need a sizeable infusion of operating cash to sustain your business before it starts turning a profit, equity investments are the only form of capital that makes sense.

When you have zero collateral

In order to take out loans, you need to have something to offer as collateral in case things don't work out quite as you planned. If you don't have anything of value to give loan providers that security, your only real option for funding is to find equity investors who are willing to take a chance on your idea with nothing to "sell" if the business goes south.

When you can't possibly bootstrap

While home-growing your company from your kitchen or spare bedroom bit by bit may not sound as glamorous as hitting the ground with investors already in your lineup, most investors will expect you to start there before they invest. But some businesses—a new automobile company like Tesla, for example— require a massive amount of capital just to get off the ground. In those cases, you have little choice but to go directly to equity.

When you're positioned for astronomical growth

Equity capital tends to follow businesses and industries that have potential for massive growth and exponential paydays. As an example, Shelli B's Sweets I mentioned above may do really well, but it doesn't have the potential to become Google, so you're not likely to attract many equity investors. On the other hand, if you're looking to build the next Starbucks chain, and you have a vision and a plan that supports that kind of growth, chances are investors will be very interested in jumping onto your bandwagon on the road to IPO.

Things to Keep in Mind

Equity narrows your options: Choosing the equity route significantly narrows your options when it comes to the future of your company. Equity investors are interested in one thing: liquidity. That means they won't be satisfied with a cut of your profits each year. Once you've accepted their money, they will expect that endgame for your business is either a sale or IPO. Before they invest in the first place, they are going to look for assurances that your idea can sell and sell big, and that that is your plan, so before you pursue the equity fundraising route, you should be sure that that is your vision as well.

Equity investors expect big rewards for big risks: If every entrepreneur could walk into a bank and get a loan to finance their idea, many probably would. Unfortunately, banks are incredibly risk-averse, and only want to provide loans that they are sure will be paid back. That's where equity investors come in: they are willing to take risks where lenders aren't. But there are two sides to that coin: an equity investor isn't looking for a simple interest payment on the money they've given you. They're exchanging more risk for more reward—a lot more—and they're going to want to see results.

Competition for equity investments is high: There are far more people looking for equity investors than there are checks being written. Most equity investors will see hundreds if not thousands of deals in a given year before they fund even one. Getting an equity investor is like getting a perfect score on your MCATs if your trying to get into medical school: you have to be in the top percentile of the top percentile of the most prepared and motivated entrepreneurs in order to be one of the few that walks away with a check in hand.

Raising equity capital takes time: No matter how prepared you are, it can easily take 3-6 months to find the right investor, and that's not counting the time it takes to complete the final legal documents that make the money available. So, if you and your business are in a time crunch, equity fundraising may not be the best way to go.

Giving up equity is a one-way street: Once you give up equity, you're not likely to ever get it back. It's very rare for an entrepreneur to buy back the equity they have given away early in the creation of their company. And once you've sold a certain percentage—let's say 25%— that's 25% of your business that you can't sell again to raise more money at a later time. Once you've sold equity to an investor, that investor is a part of your world, whether you like it or not. So as tempting as it may be to shake hands with anyone ready to write you a check, it's important to look for investors you feel comfortable having as a part of your business for years to come.

LOANS

Loan or debt-based fundraising is the easiest of the three varieties to understand in basics: you borrow money now and pay it back later, with an established rate of interest.

Debt is also the most common form of outside capital for new businesses. While angel investors and venture capitalists get all the big headlines for funding exciting companies, it's the debt providers that are behind most of the investment dollars that go into the 95% of companies that aren't splashed across magazine covers and business websites.

How it Works

When you decide to pursue debt-based fundraising, you specify in your fundraising terms the rate of interest that will come with the repayment of the loans you receive. You may also provide an expected time frame in which the loans will be repaid. These typically are structured as notes with terms of 3, 5 or 7 years.

The other important piece of the loan puzzle is collateral: some concrete, sellable thing your lenders can take from you in the event that your business goes under and you can't repay your loans. The more collateral you have, the better your chances of securing large amounts of financing.

EXAMPLE: In order to start his new furniture store, Cliff Jackson is seeking $3 million in loans, which he will use to pay for all the furniture he plans to sell. In his fundraising terms, Cliff establishes that loans will be repaid with an interest rate of 8% APR. As collateral for these loans, Cliff offers the furniture, as well as mortgage on the property for the store, which he already owns.

When to Do It

As with equity, there are a handful of scenarios where debt is the most useful option for financing your company.

When you need less than $50,000

Debt raises lend themselves well to smaller amounts of capital. At such small amounts, giving up equity doesn't make much sense anyway; and with those smaller goals there's less risk—for investors and for entrepreneurs—than when there are large sums involved.

When you need capital quickly

Is there a time-sensitive market opportunity for your business that you'll miss out on unless you raise funds now? Better not opt for equity, then—it's a notoriously time-consuming process. Debt raises tend to move along faster, giving you a better shot at getting you the funds you need when you need them.

When you need the money for a very concrete, tangible reason

If your funding needs are in the physical realm—you just need real estate, for example, or computers or other equipment— a debt raise makes a lot of sense. You'll have your collateral right there, and you'll be in position to give your investors tidy timelines.

When equity isn't available

If you aren't ready to start offering equity—or just don't want to—a debt raise may be the right course of action. Many entrepreneurs are understandably reluctant to give up equity in their company, and a straightforward debt raise has the attractive benefit of allowing you to retain ownership and control of your company.

Things to Keep in Mind

Collateral is the name of the game: Despite what you may think, banks and other lenders don't make that much profit on a single loan, especially if a few go bad. For that reason, they only say "yes" to deals where they can be 100% sure they won't lose out, and collateral is the thing that gives them that sense of security.

Lack of collateral is not the end of the world: Lack of collateral doesn't completely rule out the possibility of taking out a loan. But if you don't have any collateral and you don't plan on signing for the loan personally, your options are mostly limited to smaller loans—usually less than $50,000—that are supported by the U.S. Small Business Association (SBA). In this case, our wildly indebted yet somehow solvent government plays cosigner to your loan. Uncle Sam is a bit tight-fisted, because he has a lot of checks to hand out; but he may be the only uncle that is willing to bet on your new idea right now.
Credit is comparable: In some cases, you can achieve the same goals with credit as you can with loans, since the upper limits of both tend to be about the same for business users. American Express, for example, offers both a 30-day charge card with a floating limit and a more traditional credit card that offers flexible monthly payment options. Going with credit has the advantage that the decision is much faster compared with the lengthy loan application process. Of course, credit is going to tie back to your personal credit at some level, so if

your credit score isn't great, or you're trying to minimize personal risk as much as possible, credit isn't going to do you much good.

I remember as a young entrepreneur going into my bank Wells Fargo and borrowing $20K and sticking in a saving account at another bank. I didn't need the money for anything. In six months, I paid it back with the small amount of interest. Why? Because now Wells Fargo looked at me as a good credit risk. I then borrowed $50K and did the same thing. Pretty soon I was able to walk in and get a $100K line of credit with the same banker. I think you're getting it!

Explore your options: When considering funding possibilities, it's important to explore all of your debt options in detail to see what's available and from where. Our position with debt is this: it's always better to have financing and not need it than to need financing and not have it!

CONVERTIBLE DEBT

Convertible debt is essentially a combination of both debt and equity: you borrow money from investors with the understanding that the loan will either be repaid or turned into shares in the company at some later point in time—after an additional round of fundraising, for instance, or once the business reaches a certain valuation.

How It Works

The specifics of how the debt will be converted into equity are established at the time of the initial loan. Usually that involves some kind of incentive for investors to convert their debt into equity, such as a discount or warrant in the next round of fundraising.

If you offer investors a discount—the most common are 20% and 25% - it means that they can convert their loan into equity at that discounted rate. For example, if an investor loans you $1 million with a 25% discount in the first round, they can get $1.25 million worth in equity in the next round.

A warrant is also expressed in percentages—for example 20% warrant coverage. If we take our same $1 million case with 20% warrant coverage, the investor gets an additional $200,000 (20% of $1 million) in securities in the next round.

You will also need to set an interest rate, as you would for a straight debt raise, in order to repay your investors until they convert, as well as the investors who opt not to convert.

There is also typically a "valuation cap" for convertible debt fundraises, which is a maximum company valuation at which investors can convert their debt into equity, after which point, they will have missed the boat and will have to content themselves with having their loan repaid, or else re-invest in the company under new terms. However, in recent years more companies have been opting to leave their convertible debt offerings uncapped.

EXAMPLE: Play Store, a mobile app that reminds you when new apps are available in Google Play are about to be available, is still in development but nearing completion. The creators are hoping to raise $500,000 to complete development and make some key expansions to their staff. They've opted to follow a convertible debt structure, offering 5% interest and a 25% discount in the company's equity round next year.

When To Do It

A convertible debt fundraise makes the most sense for startups that are not yet ready to set a valuation for their company, either because it's too early to determine one, or because they have reason to believe that the valuation will be much higher at a later date.

If you believe your company's valuation is likely to skyrocket soon—but not soon enough that you can wait and do a straight equity raise at a later time— offering convertible debt has the advantage of getting you the funds you need now while enabling you to protect the value of your equity later.

Things to Keep in Mind

The best of both worlds: For investors, convertible debt offerings can be extremely attractive. For now, they have the exit strategy of the debt structure and the security that comes with it; but they also have the potential for a discount on your equity if they choose to convert. They also get a chance to watch how your business performs, allowing them to gather more information and decide whether they like where you're going before they jump on the equity train.

Or maybe not: Many investors do not look on convertible debt offerings with favor. They like knowing what percentage of a company they will own right off the bat, and they don't like taking equity - sized risks and getting debt-sized returns, even if it's just short-term. The way to sweeten the pot is by offering higher discounts so they will have the upside reward of paying less for equity than the next set of investors.

(Not) an entrepreneur's best friend: Entrepreneurs in the early stages of a startup tend to like convertible debt fundraising because it moves fast and keeps transaction costs low. But if you're committed to giving up equity, there's also something to be said for setting a company valuation from the start and starting the process of growing that valuation early on.

Know what you're doing: Because convertible debt raises are by nature a bit more open-ended than either debt or equity, if you choose to go down the convertible debt path, it's doubly important that you can provide clear reasons for that decision and a clear expectation of how things are going to shake out, both for yourself and for the investors.

Conclusion

This chapter provides just a quick overview of the three basic kinds of investor - based fundraising: equity, loans, and convertible debt. Before you commit to a structure for your fundraising, it's in your best interest to dive deeper into the specifics of that structure - or, better yet, explore each option thoroughly before committing.

Try not to get frustrated or discouraged: It's a big question to tackle, and even experienced entrepreneurs aren't comfortable with every type of capital. The more you know about your options, the stronger your position will be to make the best possible decision for yourself and for your business, and the more likely it is that your fundraising efforts will be a success.

Chapter VI
Types of Investors

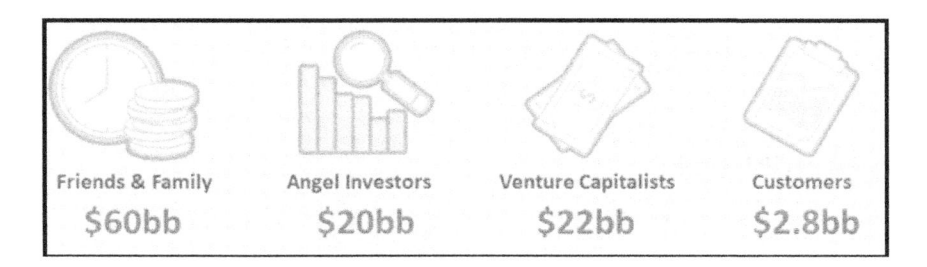

Friends & Family	Angel Investors	Venture Capitalists	Customers
$60bb	$20bb	$22bb	$2.8bb

Friends & Family

It may come as a surprise, but friends and family invest the most money in startups in aggregate, investing over $60B per year. In fact, 38% of startup founders report raising money from their friends and family. The average amount invested is about $25,000.

Seeking investments from friends and family can be an ideal way to raise seed money to get your company off the ground. This group can also be a great resource for very long-term investments, motivated more by loyalty and support than by strict return on investment. These close circles generally consist of the individuals most likely to feel a strong affinity for your brand — or, simply, to you.

However, it is of the utmost importance that all investments are thoroughly documented. You should require that they sign a document acknowledging the risk and clarifying that they may not be getting their money back. Mixing business with pleasure is notoriously risky, and for good reason. Before taking their money, do some soul-searching to be sure that your ties are strong enough to withstand the worst. By accepting their investments as you launch your company, you risk hurting your loved ones' finances. It is imperative that all parties are on the same page, literally and figuratively. Have each party sign a promissory note that spells out the repayment terms or, if you are partnering with a friend or family member, sign a partnership agreement.

Angel Investors

There are an estimated 270,000 active "angel" investors in the United States. They invest an estimated $20 Billion into 60,000 companies a year. On average, they invest $74,955 into companies – perhaps not as much as you would think.

Angel investors are high net worth individuals who invests directly into promising entrepreneurial businesses in return for stock in the companies. Many angels are successful entrepreneurs themselves, as well as corporate leaders and business professionals. Angels can be an ideal fit for start-ups, because their personal interest in the healthy growth of the business, and their own litany of past successes and failures often prompt them to act as mentor and coach to their portfolio companies. This can include introducing the entrepreneurs to potential customers and investors, identifying and advising on potential problem areas, and generally helping the startups gain credibility and recognition in their industry. As an example, Shark Tank's Kevin Harrington who spoke at my event CapitalCon is an angel investor.

Angel groups are organizations formed by individual angels interested in joining together to evaluate and invest in entrepreneurial ventures. This scenario allows angels the ability to pool their capital to make larger investments. In 2020 according to the Small Business Association, there were about 250,000 American angel investors on record in the United States providing funding for about 30,000 companies a year.

Venture Capital

There are about 1,000 active venture capital firms in the US. In 2020, VCs raised $69.1B in funding. VCs write the biggest checks of the four investor types, with an average investment size of $2.6MM to seed stage companies.

Venture capital firms are in the business of reviewing, assessing, and investing in new and emerging businesses. As a result, VCs look at a very high volume of deals, and on average only invest in 1 out of every 100 deals they consider — compared to angels, who invest in 1 out of every 10 deals. Furthermore, VCs conduct significantly more due diligence than angel investors, spending an average of 6 months on due diligence for each investment.

While angels will occasionally act as mentors to the entrepreneurs they bankroll, venture capital is consistently an active, rather than passive, form of financing. These investors seek to add value, in addition to capital, to the companies in which they invest, both to help your company grow and to achieve a greater return on their investment. This means active involvement: virtually all VCs will want a seat on the Board of Directors. The same typically applies to private equity firms who will want to take an active role.

Although most VC firms will have a website, or other means of sending in cold call solicitations, it is always best to be referred to a VC by a mutual acquaintance. This is one of the many benefits of equity crowdfunding: by asking your existing supporters to share your fundraise with their own networks, you open yourself up to the possibility of making connections that were previously thought impossible. Who knows? Maybe your sister's old high school boyfriend has a colleague who is a partner at your local venture capital firm.

Customers

In 2020, customers rallied behind their favorite companies through crowdfunding campaigns, and contributed an estimated $214.9B in total – 105% growth over 2019. The average amount of funding raised by these companies is approximately $275,000.

Crowdfunding raises rely on contributions and support from your personal and professional networks, so it is essential to develop a marketing strategy to achieve success in your crowdfunding campaign. It has been proven time and again that social media outreach is a must: for every order of magnitude increase (10, 100, 1000, 10,000) in Facebook friends, the probability of success increases drastically: from 9%, to 20%, and to 40%+. Similarly, there is a direct correlation to the number of outside links to a crowdfund and the success of the raise. It cannot be stressed enough how crucial it is for entrepreneurs to encourage not just contributions, but to also encourage their fans and followers to share it widely!

Generally speaking, the average crowdfund supporter is between the ages of 24-35 and is internet savvy. Men are much more likely to contribute to an unknown startup, and those individuals who earn more than $100,000 each year are the most avid crowdfund supporters.

Chapter VII
When do Investors Invest?

As beautiful as the world would be if any company could get any kind of capital from any kind of investor at any time, that is not the world we live in. Yet another variable in the investor funding equation is the stage of development your company is in when you decide to start fundraising.

As I mentioned briefly in the earlier Chapter III, "What Investors Look For," it's important to find investors with a history of investing in companies at the same stage that your company is currently in. These investors will know what to look for in your company, what kind of challenges you're facing, and what kind of timeline they can reasonably expect to be looking at in terms of returns, which will likely decrease the steepness of your uphill climb to earn their attention. Your company's stage of development will also determine the kinds of information you'll be in a position to give to investors, and what you'll want to emphasize on your crowdfunding profile.

For the sake of simplicity, we're going to break these stages into four basic categories: seed stage, early stage, expansion stage and late stage. For each stage, I'll touch on what companies in that stage typically look like, what kind(s) of investors usually invest at that point and what kind of fundraising may work well at that stage, as well as a few things to keep in mind about your profile. When do investors invest? Let's take a look…

SEED STAGE

The seed stage is what it sounds like: you have the "seed" of a company, but it has yet to grow into the "tree" of an actual business, although you know what kind of a tree it is and how big it is likely to grow.

Seed-stage companies typically have yet to earn any revenue and sometimes don't even have a product yet. It's important to emphasize, however, that they are NOT just ideas. If you and your buddy sit down over drinks one night and hash out a plan for the next big fast-food chain, and all you have is a few notes jotted on a cocktail napkin, you do not have a seed-stage business, nor are you ready to fundraise as such. Spend at least a few months doing market research, developing a revenue model and talking to potential customers, or risk getting laughed out of the room by investors.

Who Invests

Bootstrapping, friends and family investments, and rewards-based crowdfunding campaigns can all be great funding options for seed-stage companies.

But if you're confident that outside investors are the right choice for you right out of the starting gate, then you may want to start with angel investors. Angel investors are about equally likely to invest in a company at either the seed stage or the early stage, with around 40% of angel investments happening in each of those two stages. Angel investors tend to have been entrepreneurs themselves, meaning they understand how crucial funding can be to a business in early development. While they're certainly savvy businesspeople, angel investors are also less likely than venture capitalists to get caught up in bottom lines and profit margins and might not be as bothered by the numerous unknowns that often come attached to seed-stage investments.

Venture capitalists, on the other hand, tend not to invest at the seed stage because it's a little too, well, adventurous for them. (Remember, despite their title, venture capitalists do not enjoy taking risks.) That being said, about 7% of venture capitalist investments do come in at this stage, making this an instance when your research into the individual investor will be important. If you find a VC that has a history of investing in seed-stage companies, particularly in your industry, it may be worth a try!

How to Fundraise

In the seed stage, your best bets as far as structuring your fundraise are going to be loans and convertible debt.

At this early phase of your company's development, chances are that you don't have equity to sell yet – or, if you do, it's not worth very much, and you'll have to sell off large chunks of your business in order to get the money you need. Better to hold of on the equity round until you've built a little more momentum, and take the loan route this time around.

Or, if you're determined to start attracting equity-level attention early on, go with convertible debt: you'll still be protecting the value of your equity for now, but at the same time you'll be signaling to investors that equity – and equity-sized payoffs – are to come.

Some Thoughts About Your Profile

By definition, companies in the seed stage don't tend to have much in the way of traction. Social proof could serve as a powerful substitute there—some kind of indication that customers are excited about your product, or that you have an industry power-player in your corner.

Don't underestimate the importance of market size. Particularly if yours is a large one. Emphasize compelling statistics that you can tie directly to demand for your company's product or service. For example, if 5 billion people in the world brush their teeth every day, using an estimated 5 billion toothbrushes, and your product is a patent-protected mouth rinse endorsed by dentists that eliminates the need for toothbrushes altogether, that's a powerful piece of data that's going to show investors that there's a market for your product and, with enough funding, you're in a unique position to capture it.

This example brings up another important point: a clear, persuasive problem-solution structure sets any investor pitch and crowdfunding profile on strong footing, but in the seed stage it can be especially effective. With precious little in the way of tangible proof to nudge investors into action, convincing them that the world is incomplete without your product may be the best way to get them reaching for their check books.

EARLY STAGE

In the early stage, the "tree" is now a sapling: your company is starting to put down roots, but it's still susceptible to a cold snap or insufficient sunlight.

Early-stage companies have usually achieved at least MVP (minimum viable product), meaning their product or service is being provided to at least a small test subset of customers, and is meeting with customer approval. Early-stage companies are also often generating enough revenue to be worth talking about, although that varies from company to company.

Who Invests

The early stage is a great one for investor-based fundraising, because your chances are good with angel investors and venture capitalists alike.

As in the seed stage, around 40% of angel investments go to companies in the early stage. This means that 80% of angel investments happen at the early stage or before, so if angel investors seem like an attractive option to you and you have an early-stage company, it's a good idea to strike while the iron's hot. That being said, the early stage is also the point at which startups attract the most interest from venture capitalists. 44% of VC investments go to early-stage companies, a percentage unrivaled by any other stage. With a healthy amount of evidence that the "good idea" elevator is in fact going up, venture capitalists are going to want to get in on the ground floor – once they're sure, of course, that it's going to be worth the trip. There are many good VC and Angel Investment Groups out there – like the one ran by my friend William Podd called Landmark Angels amongst others. **(www.landmarkangels.com)**

How to Fundraise

At the early stage, there are cases to be made for all three of the investor-based fundraising structures.

With the amount of venture capitalist interest early-stage companies attract, it is a great point to pull the trigger on an equity fundraise. But if you're still feeling protective of your equity and its value, convertible debt can also be a good choice at this stage. Loans are still an option, too, especially if your company's needs run toward the more concrete and quickly repayable.

Simply put, when it comes to choosing a fundraising structure in the early stage, your options are pretty wide open, and the structure you go with will mostly depend on the other factors we discussed in more detail in Chapter V.

Some Thoughts About Your Profile

At the early stage, traction is huge. If you can prove that you've hit the ground running, that people know about your company and are already using your product or service, it will serve as a powerful indicator to investors that your business is viable, and worth their investment. *(Remember: "If they've done this much already, imagine what they can do with my money!")*

If your company is already generating revenue, be sure to talk about it: it's solid, numerical proof that you and your company have the ability to produce results. Even more importantly, show investors how their investment is going to put you in a position to generate more revenue, capture a bigger market share, create more brand awareness. When you're in the early stage, you have to be poised for growth, or else leave investors wondering where their money is going and why they should give it to you in the first place.

At the early stage, it's particularly important for investors to know what sets your company apart from, and above, the competition. Don't make the mistake of putting too many eggs in the "We're the only ones doing this" basket, either. Even if it's true that your product or service is 100% unique, to say so and then leave it at that comes off as lazy. It suggests to investors that you haven't done your research or that you don't know your industry. Lay it out for investors in concrete terms: exactly who the competition is, what those competitors are missing, and what advantage your company offers that the competition cannot possibly match. I always discuss competition as it shows I've researched the space I am in and what I am might possibly be competing against.

EXPANSION STAGE

In the expansion phase, your "tree" is getting bigger by the day and is ready to be transplanted into the big forest, where it can grow still further and compete for sunlight with other trees.

Typically, what this means in actual business terms is that you have some kind of plan in the works to grow your company – maybe you're ready to franchise your concept, or add a new product to your brand – and you need capital to make the expansion happen.

Who Invests

Interest from angel investors drops off significantly at the expansion stage, but with 18.5% of angel investments happening during an expansion, it's far from impossible to get investor support at this point.

Venture capitalists tend to like expansion more, with 26% of VC investments going to expansion-stage companies. "Growth" is a word that a lot of venture capitalists respond to, though not as much as "sale" or "IPO". If you can put those two ideas together – for example, indicate that you are expanding now in order to sell later – chances are good that you'll have a venture capitalist's attention.

How to Fundraise

You're growing! That's great! Equity investors are going to want to grow with you – again, especially if that growth is headed in a sale / IPO kind of direction.

You'll have a hard time making a case for convertible debt in the expansion phase. If your company is doing well enough to be ready to expand, investors will wonder why you're putting off giving them a share.

If you're reluctant to give up equity in order to make your expansion happen, better to go for a straight debt structure, especially if your expansion is happening in the physical realm – if you're adding new locations, for example.

Some Thoughts about Your Profile

It should go without saying that when you're in the expansion stage, the focus of your crowdfunding profile – and your pitch to investors – is going to be on your new project and how it will help your company grow.

You need to make a case for why expansion is a good idea – both for your company and for your investors. You'll want to provide research that indicates a demand for the new product among your existing customers, or for your existing product in your new market or area. Revenue projections that point to a significant increase in profits post-expansion are key, as is a clear timeline of how you see the expansion playing out.

All this being said, it's important that your profile isn't so forward-facing that it completely ignores where your company is coming from. Your past performance is crucial for inspiring confidence in investors that this expansion of yours is going to be a success. Here, again, traction is key: past revenue performance, marketing successes and customer satisfaction will all serve as proof that you know what you're doing.

Don't forget about the competitive landscape, either: whether your expansion project is going to give you the edge you need to conquer the competition, or your existing advantages make your expansion a surefire success, investors need to know where you stand, because it's where they'll stand, too, once they invest in you.

LATE STAGE

A late-stage startup "tree" has strong branches and sturdy roots and could be on its way to becoming the mightiest oak in the forest.

At this point, your company is mature and secure in its position, but that's not to say there's no reason for you to want or need to take on capital. There's a litany of reasons for late-stage companies to seek funds from investors. As the people who know your company best, it's up to you to know what your reasons are and make a strong case for them in your pitch.

Who Invests

By the time you get to the late stage, your chances of getting angel attention are pretty slim at only 2 - 4%. The odds are better with venture capitalists at 22 - 25%, but generally speaking most investors tend to have done their investing already by the time a company hits the late stage.

You can improve your odds of success by finding investors who are exceptions to the rule and have a history of investing late, or who invest in businesses in your industry or area at all different stages of development. Your chances also depend on your reasons for wanting the capital: if it's to dig yourself out of existing debt, you aren't likely to see much excitement from new investors.

How to Fundraise at this stage

Loans and equity are really the only options for late - stage fundraises and, again, the structure you go with will depend on your reasons for fundraising.

As always, loans are a good choice if your needs are concrete and not very time-intensive, or if you're not willing to give up more equity than you already have. And at the late stage, equity is definitely a solid option, especially if a sale or IPO is on the horizon.

Some Thoughts About Your Profile

By the time you get to the late stage, you should have generous amounts of traction to inspire investor confidence: strong revenues with a healthy profit margin, significant customer acceptance and social proof and, as ever, the competitive edge to prove that you aren't about to lose your market share to some upstart company with a flashy new product.

With a late - stage fundraise, it's important to be clear with your reasons for fundraising, and how investors will benefit from supporting you. You're not likely to have the same difficulties of an earlier-stage company as far as meeting with resistance for risk reasons, but big risk and big rewards often go hand in hand. If the rewards for investing in your company go down with the risks, investors may wonder if it's worth their time, and it's up to you to create a pitch, and a profile, to convince them that it definitely is.

CONCLUSION

Whatever stage your business is in when you launch your fundraising efforts, you can find the investor support that you're looking for. As we've said before, it's all about finding the investors that make sense, and choosing the fundraising structure that matches your needs and goals.

But equally important to both of these is making sure that, once you've gotten investors' attention, you're giving them the kind of information that will take them from stroking their chin to writing a check.

That's where your crowdfunding profile is a key player in your campaign. Depending on the stage your company is in – whether it seed, early, expansion, or late – there will be different kinds of information you'll be in a position to give, and different aspects of your business that you'll want to emphasize. Whatever the stage of your company, think carefully about what you have going for you, and play to those strengths in your profile. The more you do, the harder pressed investors will be to turn you down.

Chapter VIII
How to "Pitch" to Investors

In most cases, the search for investor support follows a common sequence of events. They're like stops on a subway route, and chances are you'll have to stop at each one of them on your way to funding your company – more than once, in fact. Of course, there are exceptions: a well-connected friend sets you up with a meeting, or you really do find yourself giving your elevator pitch to a high-powered venture capitalist on an elevator.

But the odds of that are similar to those of being struck by lightning, and why stake the future of your business on something as fickle as chance?

The Process of Presenting to Investors
Step 1: Research your potential investors

You compile a list of investors you'd like to work with, and that you think are likely to find your offer intriguing. Remember: the more closely the particulars of your company and your goals match previous investments an investor has made, the greater your chances of getting their attention. Remember, too, that less is often more: you're much better off contacting a few, carefully chosen investors who are actually a fit for your business than a whole army of investors who ignore you.

Step 2: The email pitch

Once you've got your list of investors ready, the next step is to reach out to them with a concise, well-crafted email. This is where you introduce yourself and your company, let the investors know that you have an investment opportunity that they might be interested in, and invite them to learn more by visiting your crowdfunding profile and/or data room - and then link them to it!

Step 3: Investors research you

If your email catches an investor's interest, they will look for ways to find out more about your company. In this day and age, that mostly involves checking out your internet presence: visiting your company website, doing a quick Google search for any press mentions or customer reviews, and looking you up on social media sites including Facebook, Twitter and LinkedIn. It also means checking out your public crowdfunding profile (which you've helpfully linked them to) in order to find out more about the particulars of what makes your business exciting from an investor's point of view.

Step 4: Investors request more info

If an investor likes what they see online, they will request more information from you— the kind that isn't publicly available to just anyone. That includes the business plan page of your crowdfunding profile, where they'll be able to see details like your revenue model and plans for future development, as well as the terms of your fundraising effort itself. They may also request other documents, like an executive summary or pitch deck. When investors request materials from you, be sure that you respond with the materials they ask for at the moment they ask for them. With every extra moment that it takes to get the information to them, you risk losing their interest.

Step 5: The in-person pitch

Everything you've done so far – the research, the email pitch, the crowdfunding profile, the executive summary – has been with the goal of getting yourself in a room with an investor to talk about your idea in more detail. If you've managed to spark an investor's interest with everything you've shown them so far, this is the point when they'll contact you to set that in-person meeting up.

The in-person pitch is easily the most important moment you'll have with the investor. Keep your pitch concise and dynamic, your pitch deck – these days, that's usually in the form of a PowerPoint presentation – minimal and free of clutter, and leave plenty of time for investor questions and discussion afterward.

Step 6: Investors request more info – a GOOD sign

You've finished your pitch, the investors seem excited—this is the part where the checkbooks come out, right? Wrong! It's the part where the investor requests more information—this time, the most detailed that you have: your full business plan, financial details, and information about who else already owns stock in your company. Don't be discouraged when investors want to know more: it means that they're excited enough about your pitch that they're willing to do the digging and due diligence to confirm that there's a real, viable company there, and not just a lot of smoke and mirrors.

Pitching the Perfect Game

It's called "pitching" for a reason: you have to get your proposal over the plate in order for investors to take a swing at it, and investors' strike zones are extremely small.

Your chances of getting your pitch into the sweet spot go up significantly when you provide investors with the right kind of information at the right time. Keep the process moving along on your end, and interested investors are likely to do the same on theirs.

The Four Types of Presentations (Pitches)

As you may have noticed, there isn't just one "pitch" when it comes to capturing investor attention: there are several. It's like laying out a trail of breadcrumbs for investors to follow, coaxing them closer and closer to investing in your company.

For the most part, drafting your various pitches is about repackaging the same information in different ways to suit each particular format. Some formats call for more information, others for less, and it's crucial to provide the right amount of information in the right format. Investors are easily scared off by too much information too early in the process. They're also easily bored, so if the right information isn't coming to them when they want it, they're more likely to move on to the next opportunity than chase after yours.

Over the next couple of sections, I'll focus on four main versions of "the pitch" to investors: the elevator pitch, the email pitch, the profile pitch, and the in-person pitch. I'll look at what goes into each of these pitches, what the goal of each pitch is, and what you can do to ensure that each version of your pitch achieves maximum impact.

ELEVATOR PITCH: The Art of being "Short and Concise"

Your "elevator pitch" is the pitch you would deliver if you ever happened to find yourself on an elevator with an investor, with just the length of that short elevator ride to get that investor interested in your idea. It's also the pitch you'd give at a party, on the subway, in the check-out line at the grocery store – anywhere you might encounter a potential investor and have a limited time frame – meaning mere seconds – in which to pitch your business.

Entrepreneurs live and die by the quality of their elevator pitches, so be ready to devote hours to drafting, scrapping, refining and finalizing yours. The good news is that there is a basic formula that successful elevator pitches tend to follow, with three essential ingredients: problem, solution and market size.

The Problem

Every great company starts by solving an important problem. The more accurately and articulately you can describe a problem, the more valuable the solution your product provides will become in the minds of your audience. And the more relatable the problem you're solving is – the greater the number of people that have encountered it, the greater the annoyance that it causes – the more your audience will wonder how they ever lived without your product in the first place.

Example: Going to the video store is a pain. People don't like traveling back and forth just to rent a movie, and they hate paying late fees even more.

The Solution

Once you've articulated a problem, the next step is to explain how your company's product or service is the elegant fix to that problem that people have been waiting for – without even knowing that they were. A good solution is a direct reflection of the problem, so it's important to tie your solution directly back to the pain points you identified while describing the problem.

Example: NetFlix provides customers with a huge selection of movies that they can have delivered right to their doorstep and never have to pay a late fee. Another observation about problems and solutions: without a clear, significant, relatable problem, your solution is a lot less compelling. The problem that you solve gives your product a sense of urgency and demand, of action that needs to be taken. Without it, your "solution" is just the one company description among thousands.

The Market Size

A clear problem and a beautiful solution are nice and all, but if the only people the problem and solution apply to are polar explorers, it's going to be hard to rustle up much enthusiasm from investors. Your market size explains how big the demand for your product is – how many people are inconvenienced by the problem, how many people will buy your product once it's available – which in turn indicates how big of a company you can build with your solution to the problem, and how much investors are going to be able to gain by investing in you.

Example: For over 90 million Americans, going to the video store is a pain. People don't like traveling back and forth just to rent a movie, and they hate paying late fees even more.

Put It Together, Then Pare It Down

Once you've articulated the problem, solution and market size clearly, the next step is to distill that explanation down to an easy-to-remember, easy-to-digest sound bite that still covers all the bases. Basically, it's about getting as much important information into the smallest number of words possible.

NetFlix helps over 90 million Americans avoid driving to the video store and racking up late fees by delivering movies directly to their doorstep, return-date free.

In a lot of cases, you'll be lucky if you get enough time to get even this short message across, so refining the message is key. Don't be afraid to go through numerous drafts. Make a few practice pitches to strangers, get some reactions and modify accordingly. It takes practice.

The Tag Line

While you personally will remember every detail of your elevator pitch, chances are that members of your advisory board and other advocates you pick up along the way won't be able to get it down flat, and investors won't remember more than a general concept.

A tag line solves that problem: it's a handful of words that gives you and others an easy way to describe your company and what you offer, not to mention a smooth intro to ease your way into the pitch. It's also a nice thing to put on your web site, your business item, your crowdfunding profile, and so on. You're building a brand, after all, and a good tag line is a great way to make your brand memorable.

Conclusion

The goal of the elevator pitch is simple: to capture the listener's interest. There's obviously not enough information there for an investor to jump straight to writing out a check, but if the elevator pitch intrigues them enough, they'll want to find out more. The better information you can get into investors' hands, the more complete the picture of your company will become in their minds, and the closer you will be to shaking hands on an investment

EMAIL PITCH: Keeping it out of the Trash Folder

The fact is that in the 21st century, most of the legwork of getting investors' attention is going to happen not in person, but in writing – starting with your introductory email. There are pros and cons to that fact: on the upside, you're able to reach out to a lot more investors a lot more quickly via email than in person; on the downside, it's a lot easier for investors to ignore you.

The addition of your crowdfunding profile to the equation takes some of the pressure off the email pitch to produce results. That being said, your email pitch still needs to be strong in order to capture investors' curiosity and nudge them toward your profile in the first place.

A good email pitch won't necessarily get you an in-person meeting with an investor, but it's definitely a step in the right direction. As with the elevator pitch, there are a few key ingredients that successful email pitches contain: a strong subject line, a personal connection, a compelling elevator pitch, intriguing company details and an enticing invitation to find out more.

Subject Line

Just like you, investors are bombarded with tons of email, and just like you, they tend to ignore a lot of it. In order to make sure your email gets opened instead of going straight into the trash folder, it's important to start with a subject line that's impossible to ignore.

It's up to you to decide what element of your company or your pitch is most likely to get an investor's attention. Maybe it's a piece of particularly impressive traction ("Company ABC growing at 200% month over month"); maybe it's your own professional background ("Company ABC, founded by former Google CTO"); maybe it's a personal connection you have with that particular investor ("Valedictorian University alumni founds Company ABC").

Whatever you decide to go with, make sure it's clear, compelling and specific to both the investor and your business. An email with the generic subject line "Investment Opportunity" – in the inbox of an investor who sees dozens of "investment opportunities" every month – is destined for the trash. The same goes for an email with a subject line that is just the name of a company the investor has never heard of and has no reason to care about.

A Personal Touch

Remember when you first started applying to jobs, and you were told to customize each cover letter you sent out for the individual business you were applying to? Introductory emails to investors work exactly the same way. In fact, if you think about it, the whole investor-seeking process looks a lot like a job search in more ways than one.

You want your first email to come off as warm, conversational and, above all, personal – not like a generic form email that is clearly going out to a whole mailing list of investor types. Address the investor by name— first name, unless you're talking to a curmudgeonly 80-year-old tycoon you think is likely to appreciate a deferential "Mr. Moneybags". Most investors have some sort of biographical information posted online. Read up, and then reference something about their history that gives you common ground: maybe you got your start in similar jobs, or maybe they gave a talk at a conference once that influenced your approach to business. If you have a direct personal connection to the investor—whether you studied under the same professor in college, have a mutual friend on Facebook or LinkedIn, or your mom was their ninth-grade math teacher— lead with that. Starting your email off with details like these establishes you as a person in the investor's mind, instead of a disembodied voice pestering them for money.

Elevator Pitch

Your elevator pitch is the heart and soul of your email, and you shouldn't be afraid to get to it as quickly as possible. Starting your email with a cold pitch may come across as forward, but a long introduction that doesn't get to the point will be equally annoying to an investor.

Don't be tempted by the change of venue from spoken pitch to written email to elaborate on your delivery, either: keep it streamlined, pared down to the bare essentials. The goal of an email pitch is still to deliver as much information in as short a space as possible, and investors will be impatient for you to get to the point.

Company Details

In the pre-crowdfunding days, your email pitch was your one real chance to hit investors with your company's traction, team and social proof – the details that transform your offer from just another harebrained scheme into a business proposition with real earning potential.

Now, of course, all of that information is included on your crowdfunding profile. But that profile doesn't do much good if you don't raise investors' interest enough to get them there, so it's still important to place a few tantalizing details in the body of your email pitch.
Brevity is still key here, so keep your details efficient, to-the-point, and fact-driven. For traction, focus on statistics that highlight your growth. With team background, stick to the experiences your team members have that are most salient to the success of your particular company. For social proof, be sure you reference individuals and institutions that investors will recognize.

Most importantly of all, be judicious and strategic the amount of detail you include in your email – don't put it all out there in the email and then have nothing in reserve to impress once investors move on to your profile.

The Ask

The conclusion of your email is where you let investors know what your fundraising goals are and what stage of fundraising you are in, as well as where they can find out more about you. It's also the part where you make a specific request for their time once they've had a chance to find out more.

The size and stage of your fundraising efforts are important indicators for investors: they tend to have minimum and maximum thresholds for their investments and invest in businesses at specific stages of development, so they'll want this information in order determine whether your offer falls in their sweet spot.

At this point, you'll also want to let investors know where they can go to find more information about your company and your fundraising: specifically, to your crowdfunding profile or data room. Include a link to it, as well as to your company website and any social media platforms you frequent – any resources that can help complete the picture of your company and what makes it a great opportunity for an investor.

When it comes to setting a timeline for getting in touch, be specific but flexible. Obviously, you want to get the ball rolling as quickly as possible, but it's important to recognize that you're more likely to meet on the investor's timeline than your own. Suggest a time frame that would work well for you as a starting point, and be ready to work with what the investor offers in return.

Starting the Conversation

The danger with the email pitch is that the investor could tune out at any second and reach for that delete button. But by the time investors have read through the entire email, they're no longer a captive audience. Your idea has

Why We're Different

Tell readers what it is about your company and its product that sets you apart from other companies and products they may have heard of or already used. Is it one-of-a-kind technology? Unbeatable customer service? Best-in-industry user interface? The more advantages you can name, the more impressive your offering will seem.

Team

This is where you provide bios of your team's key members, starting with a description of what they do for your company. Be sure to highlight past accomplishments that are relevant to your company and inspire confidence: successful launches of other startups, an impressive number of years in the industry, extensive leadership experience. And a bit of personality or humor never hurt anyone.

PRIVATE SIDE

The private, investors-only page of your profile will be far more detailed than the public side, with a lot more sections. The tone should be more business-like, while still remaining conversational. The goal is to convince investors that your company is a viable business proposition, and to push them toward inviting you for an in-person meeting — or, better yet, making the commitment to provide funds outright.

Executive Summary

The executive summary is a short, few-sentence description of your company, your vision and your goals. Describe the product or service you offer, what you have accomplished so far that makes you an attractive option for investors, and what goals the support you gain from investors will help you achieve.

Problem/Opportunity, Solution, Market Size

As you can probably tell from their labels, these sections cover the same ground as your elevator pitch. But now it's in a little more detail, and there's one important difference: it's all about the investor perspective. The thing that makes your business attractive to investors is probably different from what a customer will be interested in: a customer might be excited about your unbeatable prices; an investor would be more interested in your unbeatable profit margins. A lot of times, it's helpful to exchange the word "problem" for "opportunity: what market opportunity are you positioned to capture, and how are you going to capture it? That's what you want to address here.

Pricing & Revenue

This section provides the nuts and bolts of how your company is going to make money, and how it has made money in the past if you're already generating revenue. Charts and other graphic showing past revenue breakdowns and future income projections are powerful tools here, especially when they point to consistent and significant growth.

Competitive Landscape

Here's where you name the competition – the top three competitors is a good number to go with – and provide a breakdown of their position in the market, and their strengths and weaknesses. Then, you explain to investors how your company is positioned to blow those competitors out of the water.

Product Development

Investors like to see evidence that companies are poised for expansion and evolution. If you have any plans in the pipeline, like adding new products or moving outward into new locations, be sure to touch on them here. If possible, provide a timeline of when these expansions are likely to happen—investors will respond well to that kind of organization and laser-sharp focus.

Fundraising Terms

The bottom of the private section of your profile is where you'll detail the terms of your fundraise: the amount of capital you're seeking and the structure of your fundraise, as well as any additional details like minimum investments, valuation caps or amounts already committed.

You'll also want to provide information about the goals the money you raise will help you to achieve, and how those funds will be used. Be specific and be detailed— provide amounts or percentages whenever possible, otherwise it will seem to investors that you haven't given this fundraise much thought.

"Thank you!"

The conclusion of your profile can feel like a throwaway, but it's important to finish strong and leave investors on a note that inspires confidence and excitement. Be sure to thank investors for taking the time to read through your profile – it's a hefty amount of information, after all. Touch again on the goals that their support will help you to achieve, and how you are positioned to make their investment count. Most importantly of all, remind them that you're looking forward to being in touch again soon to discuss your deal in more detail.

Laying It All Out There

With any luck, the next time investors will be hearing about your company will be when you're in a room with them, presenting it in person. A strong crowdfunding profile or data room can nudge investors toward requesting that in-person meeting sooner rather than later. It's also an invaluable opportunity to show off your company to investors from both the customer and the investor point of view. And if it looks good from every angle, how can an investor possibly say no?

In-Person Pitch: DOs and DON'Ts

It's the finish line that every entrepreneur is hoping to cross at the end of the long, arduous race for investor attention: the in-person pitch.

Once you're in the room with an investor, it's tempting to think that the hard part's over. But there are a lot of moving parts involved in a live investor pitch, and a lot of ducks you need to have in a row. The following are some tips about common mistakes entrepreneurs tend to make in the pitch process, and how you can avoid them in yours.

DO be brief and to the point

Professional investors have a lot of decisions to make quickly, and they are famous for their short attention spans. What this means for you is that your pitch is not the time for a long-winded, involved back-story about the birth of your business. Keep your presentation under thirty minutes – including a generous amount of time for Q&A.

DO use the industry lingo

It can be daunting for those without a background in finance, but the more you talk in the language of investing, the easier it will be for investors to understand what you have to offer them. To help you with this, I've included a helpful list of common investment terms and their definitions in this guide. Study up, and not only will you be in a better position to represent your deal, but you'll be also better able to understand and answer investors' questions, too.

DON'T try to hide the risks

Making investors think you have something to hide is a poor way to kick off a business relationship. Be open about the risks associated with your business and try to anticipate any potential weaknesses an investor might notice. DON'T stop at saying what the risks are, either: detail your plan of attack for mitigating them. That kind of transparency will show investors that you've thought ahead that you're a problem solver, and that you have the ability to deal with challenges as they arise.

DON'T forget an exit strategy

Sometimes entrepreneurs are so relentlessly focused on looking for capital, they forget that investors are looking for something, too: a return on their investments. When you're pitching to an investor, don't forget to give them a clear, realistic exit plan. In other words: tell them how their investment will be rewarded, whether that's in interest or profits from sale to a larger company or an IPO scenario. A lot of entrepreneurs forget this detail, which seems tiny to them but is in fact huge for the people they're talking to.

DO be clear about what happens next

Once you've laid out all the details of your company, tell investors what you want from them, and what you're going to do once you have it. Be sure that you're clear about amount you're seeking, the terms you're offering, and how the money investors give you will be used. Be explicit, and be specific, especially when it comes to use of funds – an investor is not going to be impressed by the news that you haven't thought as far as where the money will go yet.

DO listen

When you've said your piece and it's the investors' turn to talk, keep your ears – and mind – open. Answer all their questions thoroughly and thoughtfully, no matter how many times you've heard them before, or how self-evident the answers seem to you. DON'T get defensive or interpret investors' questions as attacks on your idea or your business plan, either. If investors are asking you these questions, it's a sign that they are interested enough in your company to want to learn as much as possible before making an investment. Experienced investors know what businesses need in order to be successful, and what kinds of problems have a tendency to trip young businesses up; so, even if you don't come out of the pitch with a check in hand, an investor's feedback may teach you something valuable about how to improve your pitch, or your business itself, for the next investor you talk to.

DO be confident

Especially if your company is in early stages, your pitch may be as much about selling you as it is selling your company. The goal is to inspire confidence – both in your company and in you as an entrepreneur, leader and business partner. But there's sometimes a fine line between confidence and arrogance, and definitely DON'T be arrogant—see the above points about the importance of listening and not glossing over your weaknesses. Confidence and enthusiasm go a long way in raising capital.

DON'T neglect your business plan

Everything leading up to this– the email pitches, the crowdfunding profile, even the in-person pitch – helps to get investors' feet in the door. But a detailed, well-written, well-thought-out business plan is the thing that closes the deal on an investment. Do not make the mistake of thinking you can talk your way to an investment on charisma alone. Investors will ask to see your full business plan before they make a commitment, so when you put that document in the investor's hand at the end of your pitch, make sure it's the best representation of your company that it can possibly be.

And One Last "DO": Get Investors Excited

At the end of the day, the goal of your in-person pitch to investors is to paint a picture of a business opportunity that is simply too good to pass up. Combine powerful ideas with undeniable data, confidence and creativity with attentiveness and openness, and you will be well on your way to doing just that. As I like to say, "create FOMO – the fear of missing out on something really good."

Going the Distance

Pitching your company to investors is a marathon, not a sprint. There are more legs to this race than there are to an Olympic relay, and the fact of the matter is you may go through the process dozens of times before you get the funding that your company needs. Sometimes you will get all the way to that coveted finish line of the in-person meeting; other times, you'll drop the baton somewhere in the middle and have to start over from the beginning. Sometimes, you won't even get out of the starting gate.

The good news is that practice does make perfect, and the more times you repeat the process, the more naturally it will come to you. You'll keep discovering ways to make your pitches faster, smarter and better. You'll find the weak points that make investors hesitate, and you'll eliminate them. By the time you cross that final finish line, both you and your company will be stronger for it. And that is a victory in and of itself.

Chapter IX

Get to the Closing Table

A popular metaphor people tend to use when describing the process of negotiating investments is that of courtship – and there is a kind of wooing involved. After that first encounter the investor is largely deciding – will there ever be a second date. So far, you've flirted, you've gone on a couple of dates, there seems to be chemistry there and both sides are ready to take things to the next level.

But this is courtship in the old-fashioned sense of the word, meaning you're not just going to run off to Vegas with the girl (that's the money in this scenario). You're going to sit down with the family (the investors) and hammer out a careful marriage contract so they can sleep soundly at night knowing that their money is being well taken care of.
Just like at every other stage of the pitching process, there are "dos" and "don'ts" when it comes to closing the deal with investors. In this chapter, we'll look at some of both: the ways you can set yourself up for success, and the ways you can doom yourself to failure.

Keep Pitching

Once you've got an investor or two in the final stages of a deal, it's tempting to ease your foot off the gas on pitching to other investors and wait for those one or two possibilities to pan out. But a watched pot never boils, as they say, and one of the worst things you can do when an investor is contemplating your deal is make them feel claustrophobic about it.

So give those near-closes room to breathe, and give yourself more options by continuing to pitch to other investors. You keep busy that way, and you keep your momentum as well. Better still, if investors have the sense that you're still exploring your options, it may encourage them to move the close along more quickly on their end, to ensure that they don't get shut out of the opportunity.

Limit Your Variables

There are enough things that can cause a deal to go south on the investor's side, so do everything that you can to limit the risks on your end. When you discover aspects of your pitch that are making investors uneasy – whether you stumble on them yourself or the investors point them out to you – address those problem areas immediately. When it comes to securing your funding, you want to leave as little to chance as possible.

Focus on the Close

Closing the deal with an investor represents the conclusion of the pitch process – with that individual investor, at least. But it's also just the beginning of your relationship with that investor. So while it's tempting to rush things along and gloss over the niceties on the way to securing the check, it's absolutely essential that you keep your focus – not only so that you can be sure that all of the loose ends are tied up, but also so that you're sure that both you and the investor feel good about where things stand.

Things That Can Kill a Potential Deal

You want to believe that your romance with an investor will stand the test of time, but the truth is that even this late in the game, there are still things you can do to ruin your chances. Below are a few of the mistakes entrepreneurs make that can crash a negotiation before it even gets off the ground.

Inflexibility

It's important to remember that investment negotiations are just that – negotiations. There has to be some give and take involved, and being too uncompromising on details like minimum investment amounts, interest rates and deadlines is a quick way to cool an investor's enthusiasm for your deal.

Impatience

As eager as you are to get the money you need in the bank, keep in mind that you're more likely to be on the investor's timeline than your own. Many investors are seriously considering multiple deals at one time, and yours may not always take priority. And when it comes to considering your deal, investors do nothing hastily: the process of due diligence, research and follow-up takes months, not days. Pestering investors or pressuring them into a deal will not incline them to move any faster. Take a few deep breaths, and be ready to move forward when they are.

Unavailability

As we said before, you don't want to make investors feel rushed or crowded in the final stages of a deal. But you don't want to completely disappear on them, either. Make clear to investors that you're always available to answer any questions that come up, and at the end of each talk with an investor set a definite date for your next follow-up meeting, call or email.

Failing to ask about (and ease) investor doubts

Ask early, and ask often: "Is there anything you're not quite sure about?" Being cagey, evasive or indefinite about weak spots or uncertainties is a surefire way to scare investors off. That being said, investors understand that every investment comes with a certain amount of risk involved, and that some questions will go unanswered. So don't make answers up just for the sake of having them, and don't make promises you can't keep.

Inability to stop selling

Once you're in the habit of selling, it can be hard to stop, even when an investor is already sold on your idea. But when all that's left to close a deal is a couple of signatures, too much song-and-dance starts to come off as inauthentic and insecure. Once you know investors are committed to investing in your company, step back and just let it happen organically.

Being indefinite about the money

With all the balls you'll have in the air at this point – closing on multiple deals at once, squaring away paperwork and legal technicalities, maintaining positive relationships with the investors themselves – it's surprisingly easy to lose sight of the most important one: the money itself. Be clear with investors about when and how the money will be coming to you. Until it's in, you don't have a deal.

Rushing the process

One of biggest mistakes I see people make trying to raise money is they rush the process. Understand, nobody will invest with you until you establish trust and build a relationship. Building that requires six steps I like to refer to as The Trust Sequence. This is referenced in a wonderful book called *The Trust Economy* by Philipp K. Deikhöner.

Pedal to the Metal

When the deals are closed, the papers are signed, and the money is in the bank, you may think it's time put your feet up, relax, and congratulate yourself on a job well done.

But nothing could be farther from the truth. Now that you have the funds that you need, it's time to put that money to work! Investors want to see the good their money is doing for your company, and they want to see the chance they took on you paying off, sooner rather than later. You sold investors on your vision; now you get to give them, and yourself, the pleasure of seeing that vision become a reality.

Chapter X
Advice from Professional Investors

When it comes to understanding investors, who better to provide insight than investors themselves?

Below, some words of wisdom direct from professional investors on what you should look for when choosing investors, what you should emphasize during your pitch, and what you should keep in mind once the pitch is complete.

On Choosing Investors

Match Your Vision
"What you want is an investor whose vision for the company and expectation of what success would look like is similar to the entrepreneur's. Otherwise, you can have divergent interests and never agree and then you're almost, by definition, doomed."
Sharon Wienbar
Investor

Find Partner-Investors
"Entrepreneurs need to think quite carefully about who they take money from. Investors are partners in building your business, and you need to find people who you really want to work with, who you think can be helpful to you, who you like, who you want to spend maybe the next decade or two with. If you don't like them, if you don't think they're smart, or you don't think they can be helpful, then go find someone else."
David Hornik
Investor

Look for Investors with Different Skill Sets

"For many startups, there's really a variety of investors that might serve different needs for their company: one investor that knows about recruiting, one that knows about technology, one that knows about marketing. That also varies by stage of investment: earlier in the life cycle of a company, there's probably more need for people who know about how to build products; a little bit later, they might want to get an investor who has experience in marketing or recruiting. Further on you might want someone who has a little more scale and operational background, and at some point, hopefully, you have someone who might be able to help take the company public or arrange a sale. You're looking for a lot of different skills that will help your company, and also looking at the timing and what challenges the company might be facing in order to decide when certain investors might be more or less helpful."

Dave McClure
Founder

On Pitching to Investors

Help the Investor Understand Your Customer

"As someone who's developing a product in a certain space, you understand the customer and you understand all the little nuances about why your solution is better than the way that they currently solve that problem. Because most problems are currently being solved, it's just that there's a lot of friction in that process. So the best way to answer a question about and define the customer problem that you're solving is to really make sure that the investor understands your customer and understands exactly how they go through their daily life today, and then how you'll make it better."

Phin Barnes
Investor

The Merits of "I Don't Know"

"It's okay for an entrepreneur not to know every answer. In fact, I get really concerned when an entrepreneur claims they have all the answers. Sometimes entrepreneurs feel like they need to walk in and sell that this business doesn't have risk and that all the unknowns are answerable, and that's not the case with startups. You build credibility and you gain credibility when you are able to intelligently and coherently say: "This is what we know, and this is what we don't.'"
Josh Kopelman
Founder / Investor

The Importance of Storytelling
"The main piece of advice I give to entrepreneurs is, "Keep your eye on the prize and tell a great story." Many entreprenuers spend a lot of time giving me excruciating details: about their products, about how they're going to operate from Monday through Saturday. But they don't really tell a great story. So I tell them to become a good storyteller. They're going to need that to give their pitch; they're going to need that to recruit their employees; they're going to need that to convince customers to buy products from them when they're a brand new company. My most important piece of advice is, "Become a great storyteller, and make sure that the story has a big happy ending.'"
Ann Winblad
Founder

Be Coachable
"As an early stage investor, I'm not looking for somebody who's got all of the skills to build and develop a company. What I'm looking for is somebody who's got the passion and commitment to put in the hard work, but is also willing to listen to the advice I've got to give. I'm looking for someone who's coachable – not somebody who's going to do what I say without question, but somebody who's at least going to listen to the mistakes that I've made, so that they don't go and make those same mistakes."
Nelson Gray
Angel Investor

What Happens After the Pitch

How to Gauge Investor Interest
"It's very difficult to understand sometimes: did you get a yes, or did you get a maybe, or did you get a soft no? Usually if investors are interested, they'll say by the end of the meeting whether they want to have another meeting. If they say, 'Let's follow up,' that's not such a clear signal. If they say, 'Let's arrange a meeting, talk to my assistant about scheduling it,' then that's probably real interest. If you haven't heard from them, it doesn't mean that they're not interested – they might just be busy. But if you've been blown off two or three times, you might want to prioritize other investors who are engaging with you over that other person. Certainly, you can get to a point where too much pressure on them will turn a 'maybe' into a 'no' rather than a "yes".
Dave McClure
Founder

Know There's a Route to the Money
"As an entrepreneur, you need to ask as part of your first meeting, 'What is the process here? What happens next?' 'What is the route to your wallet?' is the question you're asking. If the venture capitalist can't give you an answer to that, you probably should go find another venture capitalist. You'll be spending all of your energy during the pitch process, and you need to know that there is a route to the money with every venture capitalist that you're pitching to."
Ann Winblad
Investor

Don't Be Desperate

"Frequently, entrepreneurs, during due diligence, go down the drain because they show urgency, they show that they're desperate, and that they're really counting on us. Entrepreneurs need to show that they have other options and the ability to walk away, so we don't think that we're their only option. Some of the worst decisions we've made have occurred when we really liked the entrepreneur and we knew that we were the only option they had to pursue their dream. We should have asked ourselves, 'I wonder why we were the only ones who loved this idea and loved this team?'"
John Huston
Founder

Fail Well

"Does failure matter? It depends how you failed and why you failed. If you're going to fail, you fail in the way that causes the least damage to your personal reputation and to the reputations and wallets of your investors. If you have a good failure, then you'll get backed again. If you fail because you failed to listen to your investors, or you were unable to react to obvious market changes, then failure is a bad thing and you're not going to get backed again."
Nelson Gray
Angel Investor

Chapter XI

Industry Terminology – Things to Know

During your fundraising, you want investors to focus on learning about you and your company, not struggling to understand what it is that you want, or what you have to offer them in return. That's why it's crucial that you be able to discuss your company and the opportunity it presents to investors in terms that investors will understand.

That's not a problem if you've gone through the investment process before, or if you have a strong background in finance. For a lot of people, though, it can take a bit of studying up. To help you out with this, I've compiled a list of **common investor terms** you hear often in the investor world, along with an easy-to-understand definition for each.

* * *

Acquisition: When a larger company—for example, an Apple or an Amazon — purchases a controlling interest in your company, that larger company has acquired your company. Acquisition by a larger company is a common goal for startups pursuing equity campaigns.

Add-on services: Assistance an investor may provide to your company aside from their monetary contribution— for example, making introductions to other investors, helping to assemble a management team or helping to prepare for an IPO.

Benchmarks: Performance goals used to measure the success of a company. Many investors use certain benchmarks – for example, yearly revenue or yearly increase in sales – to decide whether a company merits additional funding.

Buyout: The purchase of either a company or a controlling interest in a company's shares or business. A buyout is often the long-term goal of startups and other businesses pursuing equity fundraise campaigns.

Board of directors: A group of people elected to act as representatives of the stockholders in a company. Members of the board of directors handle management-related policies and make decisions regarding major company issues, including the hiring/firing of executives, options policies and executive compensations. The board of directors should fairly balance the interests of both management and shareholders alike.

Cap table: Short for the "Capitalization Table", a cap table is a detailed list of exactly how much stock each entity or person owns. Think of it like a spreadsheet that simply lists names and percentage ownership stakes, all adding up to 100%.

Common vs. preferred stock: There are many "classes" of stock that can be issued in a company, and each class may have its own rights and preferences. Investors typically get preferred stock, which may give them preferences such as the ability to get their investment back first, before the rest of the common stock holders get their proceeds. Founders and employees are usually left with common stock, which means they're usually the last people to get paid.

Convertible note: A convertible note is a loan made to a company that can be converted into stock by the choice of the issuer or holder at certain events. Each note has an interest rate, a maturity date, and may come with the option to convert at a discount at a future round or time.

Dilution: The effect of giving someone else part of the company's stock is considered "dilution". It means that you are diluting your equity stake to make room for someone else. When you're worried about "giving away the company", what you're worried about is the dilution of your company.

Drag along rights: Designed to protect the majority shareholder in a company, drag-along rights enable a majority shareholder to force a minority shareholder to agree to the sale of a company. The majority owner is required to give the minority shareholder the same price, terms and conditions as any other seller, with the goal of eliminating minority owners and securing 100% of the company's stocks to the buyer.

Due diligence: The process of investigation and evaluation of the details of a company, which investors complete before they make the final decision whether to invest in that company.

Exit strategy: the means by which an investor "cashes out" of an investment and earns the return on investment that they are seeking in making the investment in the first place. Typical exit strategies include IPO, acquisition and buyout. Also known as a "harvest strategy" or "liquidity event".

Follow-on investment: An additional investment made by an investor who has already invested in a company, typically made once the company is at a later stage of development.

Initial public offering: Commonly abbreviated as IPO, is the first time that stock in a private company is made available to the public. An IPO is a common goal for startups pursuing equity campaigns.

Return on investment: or ROI, is the profit or loss resulting from an investment. It's typically expressed in terms of a percentage. For example, if an investor makes a $100,000 investment in a company and gains $2 million when the company is acquired by a larger company, that's an ROI of 200%.

Risk: the likelihood of loss or less-than-expected returns, including the possibility of losing some or all of the initial investment. Risk is typically quantified using the historical returns or average returns for a specific investment.

Seed capital: The first round of capital that is put into a business, typically coming from the company founder and friends and family. Seed capital comes before any large investment rounds have been taken on, often during the pre- or low-revenue stages of a company. The capital is typically used to help build traction in order to attract attention from venture capitalists in later stages of fundraising.

Stock option pool: When a company takes on an investment, the investor will usually request (or, more accurately, insist) that you allocate a certain percentage of the company's shares to a Stock Option Pool for future employees. That pool comes out of your portion of the stock, not the investors. Stock option pools will range from as little as 5 points of equity to as much as 20 points.

Term sheet: A non-binding outline of the terms and conditions according to which an investment is to be made—for example, the interest rate of a debt investment, or the valuation for equity. It's similar to a Letter of Intent in that it indicates a strong interest to move forward, but it's not the same as guaranteeing an actual deal gets done.

Valuation: An estimation of what your company is worth at a given point in time. While you may be the person who sets the valuation of your company, until an investor agrees to that valuation, and writes a check based on that valuation, it's not validated.
Pre-money valuation is how much the company is worth before the investor puts money into your company. So if you set your valuation to be $2 million, and the angel investor puts in $500,000, your pre-money valuation is $2 million.

Post-money valuation is how much the company is worth after the angel investor puts money into your company. So if you set your valuation to be $2 million, and the angel investor puts in $500,000, your post-money valuation is $2.5 million.

Vesting: a process by which you "earn" your stock over time, much like you earn your salary. The purpose of vesting is to grant stock to people over a fixed period of time so they have an incentive to stick around. A typical vesting period for an employee or
Founder might be 3 – 4 years, which would mean they would earn 25% of their stock each year over a 4 year period. If they leave early, the unvested portion returns back to the company.

* * *

The Least You Need to Know

It's the investors' job to be the expert about investing; it's your job to be the expert about your company. You don't have to be an investment genius in order to get investors excited about your opportunity. But the more familiar you are with these common investor buzzwords and their meanings, the better situated you will be to represent what you have to offer, field investors' questions, and keep the whole process moving surely and smoothly toward that end goal of getting your company the funding it needs.